Gloss

Giles Goodland

Newton-le-Willows

Published in the United Kingdom in 2012
by The Knives Forks And Spoons Press,
122 Birley Street,
Newton-le-Willows,
Merseyside,
WA12 9UN.

ISBN 978-1-907812-76-7

Copyright © Giles Goodland, 2012.

The right of Giles Goodland to be identified as the author of this work has been asserted by him in accordance with the Copyrights, Designs and Patents act of 1988. All rights reserved. No part of this publication may be reproduced, stored in a retrieval system, transmitted in any form or by any means, electronic, photocopying, recording or otherwise, without prior permission of the publisher.

Acknowledgments:

Lines, sections, and individual words from this poem have previously appeared in Filling Station, Foma & Fontanelles, and as part of a group poem in Painted, Spoken. A substantial extract from the poem appeared as a chapbook in the Dusie 5th Kollektiv, 2011, under the title 'from Gloss'.

Gloss

Aaa, doming deust.
Ab, and onanism.
Abacurse, anathematic sumation.
Abridgestract, twoarched subpension.
Abscene, primeal screan.
Achery, fletcherous bownpain.
Achinery, pistonish meanchism.
Achtongue, illiterative prosembody.
Acrobot, strainless grimnast.
Acronysm, inertial fletters.
Adjustify, means ends.
Admisinter, burlied sembody.
Adverge, greynoisy surrepetition.
Aeligature, ajointed crocagile.

Aetherplane, areal bardment.
Afflautist, mausical berather.
Afternoone, untry landescape.
Agenaut, altirrational trancestor.
Aghainst, doppelganged herror.
Agrain, corngested sereal.
Agrainst, upposable harnds.
Airbone, swinged tomarrow.
Airear, eagless raravis.
Airticle, ministring clould.
Ajangle, quiverb reverate.
Alassitude, weakly rarecline.
Alcohole, babysmal deapth.
Alcoholly, plumpud celeberation.
Alexicon, golossal chancelist.
Alfabeti, bolognical lasagnage.
Aliment, perhapsor elemeant.
Allossary, catacosmic boneyard.
Alossary, azead listwards.
Alseep, astirred invertor.
Altopiece, conclasted shring.
Amchine, petallic selflist.
Amethystle, dreamencased crustal.
Amotion, heynonnynovative meadowlarkin.
Amusicologist, humboned earroar.
Anager, humun esources.
Anarchive, unmaginable corepus.
Andstorm, s s.
Anecdont, farbidden divistory.
Angeless, mangerial revelution.

Angerangel, crossgroined mangager.
Anglexicon, archadamic databasemen.
Anglosaxophone, impoverised glossolo.
Animalasm, feelery nodething.
Animalism, ganglioned demiurge.
Aniquity, unscient forehest.
Anrrow, withless projectrial.
Antcester, porevious insectide.
Antenational, protofocal tribolite.
Antenebrae, dustiful shouldows.
Antidictionary, exiconic wordlest.
Antimate, deautiful golover.
Antimations, of emortality.
Antmusic, postadamic choreality.
Anuthor, shelfmade halterity.
Aparallel, un eyeverse.
Aparticle, storange atomb.
Apressex, tristy postcogitus.
Aqualune, aqualude aqualung.
Arcrobat, alithe entancer.
Arcross, starloft unstellation.
Arepresent, anauthor isvisible.
Arist, tit-led hipocracy.
Armputee, wartimid victime.
Artoffice, ifficial drealism.
Arvoparticle, tinabulare mote.
Asbestoast, sinsliced beread.
Asdust, sootable ashtone.
Asheep, burntoff erring.
Ashh, farced asleap.

Assassinsect, cultcellular terrormite.
Asscent, of man.
Assembulance, caremergent redoctor.
Assetstrip, agrainst quantichrist.
Asunderstood, emusculate antibodily.
Atishoot, sneased gurnunner.
Atlist, atlost atlast.
Atomato, rubish invegitation.
Atomb, sepulchritudinous tearminus.
Atomsphere, nucellar poretection.
Auncle, kinfold unaunt.
Autanimation, cartuned workflow.
Autherror, plathetic suincide.
Autm, elategrown halvest.
Autom, imagic ommage.
Automan, careparing timechanic.
Automanual, car handbook.
Automata, carscarred melanchasms.
Automatom, selfsame articule.
Automatum, endgendured firmameat.
Automnal, tumated trumnet.
Automnate, affordist selfassembly.
Automnation, belate carpital.
Autumnation, robooted leafilm.
Automoney, untilled ashmachine.
Automoon, suspent mashiner.
Autopia, carhinged maninfestation.
Autostell, pinnumbered cashcade.
Autumnail, summered moonclip.
Autumnate, ignatural faungus.

Autumnatism, fallable extinglishment.
Autumnative, cashtille sleptimbre.
Autumnature, treemorsed sapfall.
Autumnest, sleeptimbre's crumbfort.
Autumnobile, carring crumbustion.
Autumnonmoon, silverside nilclipping.
Autumnoon, mildayed massdial.
Autumnoonmoon, fiantly devisible.
Autumoney, quantive earsing.
Autumony, seminatural hypernation.
Autumoomn, sleafless owliness.
Autumoon, gloden sophere.
Avantgardigan, costpoital reversear.
Avernue, eastly descert.
Aviolator, eerial ravatar.
Awking, wideaway draymare.
Awkword, bearbaric revocable.
Aword, vocab lelexeme.
Axexamine, onelithic astoneage.
Azebra, bestural zoolist.
Azutumn, blurmembered palearctic.

B

Baalistic, intercontent hittile.
Baldelaire, ploems maudits.
Bambooze, tristilled iquor.
Barbarbary, blackship forthmaster.
Beareth, sighsized airfall.
Becamera, shutterly eyeself.
Bedside, be beside.
Bee, lined matchmaker.
Beeleaf, treed alightly.
Beerwolf, beakering meadator.
Beestmilk, bestfled measting.
Beestory, apic disdance.
Beetatest, gonelive hiversion.

Beeyond, be leaf.
Behemoth, be she-moth.
Behindmoth, agolemic urversion.
Beholed, worndown shredsheet.
Behomian, angleheaded beautnik.
Belabeast, termitten workant.
Beleaver, erreligious nonvert.
Belettle, illaterate litrism.
Bellybone, umbellic stoneache.
Belowgrounderground, subtrainian intunnel.
Bemoth, assail wingedly.
Bereather, lunguish expiray.
Beshemoth, fadylike monastar.
Besmother, whinged lungstop.
Bestuary, delterious ebbeing.
Betailion, beeheaded eetle.
Betatest, supprovisional dustrial.
Betaversion, imengined illquipment.
Bewilderness, ereabouts unknow.
Bibel, velluminous detextbook.
Bilography, atonymous dungsroman.
Biolognese, frothcoming antinature.
Bired, foulegged firend.
Birthdeath, wakesleep herethere.
Blestuary, allustrated riverend.
Blistear, lymphing skinflection.
Bloodcolt, blolted foall.
Bloodletter, redeaded deathsent.
Blossbomb, folowery blubble.
Blossomb, cloured folower.

Blossomber, faerial wreather.
Blossumation, fritful blueberriness.
Blubble, rubberst bloon.
Bluer, embe redhills.
Bodyhood, pretensile eyielid.
Boeing, beoing bone.
Bohemoth, grooven wingbeatnik.
Bonerung, sladdery deascent.
Bonyfriend, armorous ramourer.
Bookinsect, pageworn leaflest.
Bookself, oluminous ursona.
Bookworn, thereaded eyeself.
Brainloss, cerebrate ament.
Brainside, cuppable meantality.
Brainworn, readbare headworm.
Breathborn, respired etherend.
Breathlass, flowlowing melady.
Breathlist, eareal bardment.
Breathloss, lungeless enchancer.
Breathren, belunging otherhood.
Breathtake, inchaled lungfurl.
Britand, uketc englandsoon.
Brokend, mirr orrimmage.
Bulbocity, huburban evelopment.
Bullblubber, glaseal wallrush.
Burntable, urnable turnbabble.
Businessmen, of Kalahari.
Butterful, behinged shutterfly.
Bybyproduct, reffluent mischarge.

C

Cabalage, cruciferal kohlrabbi.
Caballage, talmuddy coleword.
Cabbalage, rotunded tractation.
Cabballage, vegetable plot.
Cabcharge, timetered cargone.
Calmour, franquil chasis.
Camerangle, malgazed pointofyou.
Can, not opener.
Canopera, longsung solung.
Canvast, opale ustration.
Capitalisman, fetish object.
Car, avant caravan.
Caralarm, coralarm carolarm.
Caralarmer, malarming encalment.

Caralarmist, airworn mallarmery.
Carapaced, persplex protext.
Carash, emotor ancident.
Caravarn, avernous terailer.
Caravern, vacavant infrill.
Carbody, shieldead boneness.
Carbom, blastic entrapmeat.
Carbone, exoskeletal deriver.
Carbonnet, hingecase tripoint.
Carborne, autumotive trainsport.
Carbuckle, surcling chaingear.
Carburn, new trail.
Carcancer, disrusted carcinema.
Carcarash, ancidental causalty.
Carcaress, uncased predestrian.
Carcase, pietalic bonebody.
Carcinoma, tumidst carceration.
Carcrush, jambed motornway.
Cardriver, filindexed camuter.
Carelease, tamporary findigit.
Caremember, ductrecalled bloodypart.
Carescape, cemetarry corrodeblock.
Carface, surficed chaingangster.
Carful, jambacked scaredhead.
Cargone, untacked debody.
Carhenge, unscient homument.
Carhere, oillwill sumpwhere.
Carhire, rustworth noretail.
Caringene, predestrian timechanic.
Carlarmity, illmelt metalphor.

Carline, scarry illside.
Carmake, etalic remarque.
Carmalade, traffic jam.
Carmen, blurban derivers.
Carmine, owned vesickle.
Carnation, chainchristian ceremoney.
Carnivortext, selfeating meatfiction.
Carolarm, coralarm earalarm.
Carroll, carrock carwreck.
Carollery, corrollary dorollery.
Carorvan, heavely ransport.
Carosion, derosive corrustion.
Carpart, scarpmental merchance.
Carpetal, flooral desing.
Carpool, frogmantic carppound.
Carrage, crossrowed estranger.
Carrageway, corrodeway dualitway.
Carrouse, dissipant emachination.
Carseat, meatalic effuelent.
Carsick, imachinary illectricity.
Cartease, gocentric cogitow.
Caruser, suprising commutiny.
Carvacuum, whovering breathtake.
Carworn, huneard oilsive.
Carzone, motorn odeway.
Cashtille, rows of.
Castaract, idistinct materfall.
Cavernacle, shriney mountinside.
Cawmotion, descare crow.
Ceanographer, atery etacean.

Ceasesleep, seasleep seesleap.
Celement, hearden atomb.
Cementia, crumblink moretice.
Cemetarry, eepest midnought.
Centrails, gastrointentional inwords.
Centrifugue, canticular plansong.
Centurals, mtnous timelaya.
Cerebellion, dishordered commutiny.
Cervices, crevices vertices.
Ch, ambercham ber.
Changed, chanced utterly.
Chaosm, covernous deapth.
Chaosmonaut, astar raveller.
Chasmism, labysmal atlantissue.
Chelm, dubbled utch.
Chemtrail, sensored eyevolve.
Childerness, revoloving playgoround.
Childlish, bablong kidlingo.
Childream, cylintered creamation.
Childwho, imagained clandestiny.
Chilld, midly innosensible.
Chipbooks, poemes frites.
Choicean, illexical periment.
Cholice, wholey greal.
Chronicicle, ignordic sungsaga.
Cinemact, prefabulated dreama.
Cineman, camerantic inflick.
Cinemass, seecremental urvice.
Cirrosive, alkative bringe.
Clacklack, lucklaster licklock.

Clanguage, evocational clongeur.
Clatteract, ushpring waterflaw.
Clatterclysm, maintainous ravelanch.
Clauseway, nonjunctive sentensation.
Clicklock, fasturned deeposit.
Clifff, oresho resea.
Clockfall, zeroing midnought.
Clocklet, audenary wystwatch.
Clocksure, ourly meminder.
Clockwalk, menachanical crowbot.
Clockword, speaken tocktrick.
Cloudloud, raincloven forknife.
Clung, longated ung.
Coalchemist, fossuelled ageologist.
Cobbing, boblonian bablarian.
Codefine, descrypted infinition.
Coherenet, mutrual coillustration.
Coinception, cogitus interruptus.
Colould, bedruggled consumee.
Combone, museful imprement.
Comeant, apsteroid crimeteor.
Comeat, ashteroid dimeteor.
Comelette, ashterror hometier.
Comelt, ashtrayed meatear.
Comeltear, astavoid meattear.
Comelteor, asteroyed meateor.
Comemoth, astray meatephor.
Coment, astremote meatore.
Comenteor, astroyed meltier.
Cometary, cacasteroid memoteor.

Cometear, casteroid metalphor.
Cometeor, catasteroid metameteor.
Cometh, corticosteroid metastar.
Cometime, desteroid meteorm.
Cometo, disasteroid metephor.
Cometory, easteroid meterror.
Cometose, fasteroid metier.
Comettear, hasteroid metobe.
Comit, masteroid metorn.
Comlet, onsteroid moreto.
Comment, pasteroid moterror.
Commet, staroid remoteor.
Commetary, stearoid remoter.
Commetiny, ursteroid timear.
Commit, usteroid timetear.
Comote, vasteroid timeteor.
Comoth, wasteroid timetier.
Condem, semi nation.
Concreation, rustalizing stonement.
Consciousness, of stream.
Consumee, corpsrate deadvertment.
Consumeree, urchased undividual.
Consumeria, delixirious hoppingmal.
Contradictionary, lexiclastic dialexis.
Coole, Wilde's ones.
Copaceous, fallacial seathrough.
Coquetteaser, sirable osiren.
Corepirate, assailing privatear.
Coretext, decentral nocument.
Corevalue, unstitutional odeology.

Cornear, caracted eyesphere.
Corruporate, leveraged buryout.
Corruporation, nobodied saciety.
Cosemic, athematic unireverse.
Cosmist, misteyed castronomer.
Cosmosis, insidereal spacies.
Counterclock, irreverse timebone.
Couplimb, twobacked fourlegs.
Coyoterie, doggend woofpack.
Crablouse, small infestor.
Crabstract, sphincered clawtrack.
Crackery, bonechinese tablewore.
Crawmotion, rookarised teetrop.
Creapture, depthly ergency.
Creptomania, lopshifting shelfabuse.
Creviced, cerviced vertice.
Crimsonset, daylung disippearance.
Crocagile, robatic preditor.
Crodicil, addended allegator.
Cromeant, eateroid metephor.
Crowmotion, berling airlife.
Cryptofacets, uniformighty forkfolk.
Crystallion, sequine diamount.
Cubeast, nodescending stairplane.
Culdeshack, dunken ruinn.
Cupicle, curtinted urtorns.
Curelty, blassed medisong.
Curemember, doctorn riversion.
Curflew, cturnal subsensong.
Curtainty, shrouded trusth.

Cutout, them iddlemen.
Cword, seaworn sexpression.
Cycalone, oneyed vortext.

D

Dadad, deadead decessor.
Dadata, antistatistic memorandom.
Dalektrician, exterminal plositivist.
Dancestor, imprevious plast.
Dancestore, innarational misinterest.
Dancestory, breathborn flowship.
Darmth, summermid nightdimmer.
Dataist, dissociated vangardian.
Datamancer, orbitten actioneer.
Datasonata, intanglable corposition.
Daydrum, nonotonous inflex.
Daylung, breatholess sealight.
Dead, see scroll.

Deadend, erminal culdeshack.
Deadlet, prediseased curpse.
Deadleye, belind arksman.
Deadream, awking nightmoor.
Deadult, deseized unkid.
Deadvertise, cromercial unformation.
Deafend, blearyeared hearring.
Dearm, disremembered bonewish.
Dearthread, spiderspun intwine.
Deathbreath, thearts threadsbreadth.
Deathred, infateful scission.
Deathshed, overnous ashamber.
Debatabase, negatiable corposition.
Debituary, inthered destatement.
Decembed, rimed windhours.
Decembud, tinearly ingrowth.
Decrease, fulllength morrir.
Deeposition, wormward gestimonial.
Deepriver, uffordable taxonation.
Deerode, ogressively reteriorate.
Defignition, glossal planation.
Defignote, ignorite glossover.
Defignotion, preplosive explonation.
Defigure, oremove icthures.
Definery, respectacular enclothing.
Definity, ubjective insideity.
Definotion, unimanageable gloss.
Deifiled, hunoly defecration.
Delaughter, offsprung scenedance.
Deleuzery, rhymezomatic doppelgangler.

Delfinition, glossoly anchord.
Delfinotion, idereal hypnothesis.
Deliquency, folowing renager.
Deliveroil, efishent coldiver.
Demicolon, pariodic fillstop.
Demonstraight, forkhorned dedeity.
Dentangle, overbrushed treefall.
Deprose, lilyrical pomposition.
Derevelation, riverdriven siltslit.
Dervil, dangeloud descendance.
Descendancer, arcrobotic springoff.
Descentaur, stalleonine mancestor.
Desing, illyric unverse.
Despond, refringed acheland.
Despondunce, middenaged sumpthing.
Despositism, fedgehund entropiary.
Dessurrection, martiring birthdeath.
Detestament, villonous confestion.
Dethreadul, unseamly clothure.
Detonotation, semitextual ingnition.
Diamonad, crystaleyed indivisible.
Diamonand, glashard uninut.
Diamound, listery treassure.
Dictatorphone, staling mussoline.
Dimlight, midnaut amidnit.
Dimminish, unset twiglight.
Dimsister, cobwebbed sornority.
Dimslit, candly furhole.
Dimstant, starstirred heedlights.
Dingalinguist, lalabelled amusicologist.

Diremond, crystale gelobe.
Dirtionary, desoiled thearthbook.
Disdust, remoted unbeam.
Diseasiness, undistentang lable.
Disfinger, aremoved findigit.
Disghost, exponge spurit.
Disharm, sunking supsoap.
Disinflect, asterilized worldist.
Disintlerest, unearthling thou.
Dismayland, the mepark.
Disnetangle, uncumber clochely.
Disorderer, caostic entroppler.
Disremember, interful orget.
Disrememberment, illforgotten grains.
Dissonata, ursonant pianoepic.
Distrance, farstaring nockturn.
Divivision, splitered enclove.
Dlaughter, eautiful offerspring.
Dogend, armend legend.
Dolloll, lollopen deroller.
Dollover, limpless mannerkin.
Doormant, dustiful waityer.
Doppelgang, twining opposight.
Dourway, behinged endrance.
Drainbow, ridescent puddoil.
Dreadend, martal treecoil.
Dreadevil, skeery manstunt.
Dreama, trunslated indentity.
Dreamadam, everie riverie.
Dreamand, persond reamed.

Dreamander, onearic amland.
Dreamare, sharkly descentaur.
Dreamature, auromatic alsoran.
Dreambassade, knightly visector.
Dreambassador, fureign consoul.
Dreamber, wavebone antsealant.
Dreambery, wavebone antsealant.
Dreambic, pent ammeter.
Dreambience, atomspherical orboist.
Dreambition, spirational breathole.
Dreambone, muscical elatone.
Dreambonehead, skulful headcore.
Dreambook, looseleft nockjournal.
Dreambulance, mergency nonveyance.
Dreambush, latigued furprising.
Dreambushed, revisioned urprise.
Dreamdemeaning, leaningmess faltower.
Dreamdrum, mononotonous downbeath.
Dreameaning, unterpretal apsense.
Dreameat, injested mareflesh.
Dreameditor, unshore nonproof.
Dreamerica, braven e-world.
Dreamerican, ravenew orld.
Dreamericanical, childhooded dismayland.
Dreamhead, nervelastic dumbfound.
Dreamhole, misting pliece.
Dreamist, blureyed tractitioner.
Dreamlifeboat, unsthinkable seekraft.
Dreamloss, wakeless murning.
Dreamother, ulternate matriline.

Dreamputate, delimbing dwindleg.
Dreamself, sleepshaped mindhole.
Dreamsinger, henrician ferryman.
Dreamslaughter, innered viscion.
Dreamslinger, edornian museteer.
Dreamsong, hormonious nockturn.
Dreamsonnet, hemical drealism.
Dreamutter, evocalise seamingly.
Drecember, cricketrung glasshour.
Drudgeon, etymonastic excographer.
Duskrose, darkend efflower.
Dusteye, moted organlid.
Dustfall, postunclear shunset.
Dustill, furnal rustingplace.
Dustillery, shelfish librarity.
Dustrealism, autopian architexture.
Dustrust, dural carageway.
Dwindliness, wastaway sappearance.

E

Eagleness, eyrial talont.
Eagless, raptorn emptinest.
Eangle, tangular rapturn.
Earalarm, ingotten langaugh.
Earbeat, herent intinnitus.
Earcohole, verberating listender.
Earfeel, everberant longonge.
Earfelt, heardend sunsound.
Earhole, clugged porthal.
Earicular, cornfessional scarement.
Earpeeling, spiracular dispear.
Earplane, humman playode.
Earroar, tinnightly overberation.

Earsehole, golistening archamber.
Earshell, egglistening pearlobe.
Earteat, fleshlit pinipple.
Earthbreath, birdsigh windhove.
Earthbreathe, disembodily ephemerald.
Earthear, frungal uricle.
Eartheatre, tyradio gedy.
Eartheth, shonehenge hillfigure.
Earthole, untainside cavacuum.
Earthread, tunely unwind.
Earthred, arrative shoryline.
Earthrent, thretend catastroy.
Earthrob, tympanic erroar.
Earthrobe, everbereating tinnotion.
Earththrob, thistless depillage.
Earthwarm, summering crumboil.
Earthwarn, acherubbed theomorph.
Earthwax, wornown andle.
Earthwormswarm, viviscid serpentangle.
Earthworn, valleyed scurface.
Earvestment, trombine hairvista.
Earworm, respetitive harmelody.
Eat, esteamed vegotable.
Eather, hairial cholice.
Eavesdrip, adammed gogutter.
Ebbeing, betidal estarry.
Echole, ess ess.
Echorecho, reverbal undersounder.
Echtoplasm, hostly coalessence.
Eerywhere, allovery evertingle.

Effair, extramaritual hedventure.
Effiguy, fawlksy burnaround.
Eggcyst, ovoided chambearth.
Eitheror, oneor theother.
Elationship, bodilying dalliaison.
Elemelt, meatomic soupson.
Elergy, longhost deode.
Eleton, areboned corupse.
Elist, fuor quarkets.
Elmement, woden strunk.
Elonglost, lusive lhost.
Elsehere, placeless interject.
Emberess, glowred rescinder.
Embodimelt, dissapainting eleton.
Embryodiment, eveloped forfeitus.
Embryody, flooting amnyone.
Emergy, joyfall incidement.
Emotorway, deriven superformance.
Enchaintment, slurgical rickery.
Enchantorment, brewitched spiell.
Endangermanagement, therepied temperor.
Endlessnessless, eaturnal retrun.
Ends, justiffy meands.
Energineer, machinical electrice.
Enigmachine, deusex china.
Enjoymen, sensural leasurers.
Enought, ifficient surpulse.
Entanglanguage, adamented seamonstress.
Entombations, of faltality.
Entorpy, enunding nonthing.

Entropery, everentual flufillment.
Epiphoneme, sourrounding earfeel.
Erotorogeny, mountainted sinkline.
Erspent, eelong enadder.
Escaperope, o pening.
Escapescape, exitentual eggression.
Estar, emporal satate.
Estatuary, orchitectural effiguys.
Estatue, marbleyed faunymph.
Etcetacean, everending whalesolong.
Etcetarian, whalesung searia.
Etceterrestrial, tentacling andsoon.
Eternatural, evereveried entropiary.
Etext, virtureal plage.
Ethistle, airmailed overseed.
Eunough, ballless castaract.
Eveling, elevening valein.
Evereverie, nerverending sundaydream.
Evereverse, reternal servorance.
Everevolve, macadamic insusserection.
Everlation, nontemporary veinsight.
Everope, selfaddress colletter.
Eviary, birdwide acrage.
Excesslessness, moterate wifestile.
Exexile, reinturned efugee.
Exlexile, rereturned fugee.
Eyears, vertile timepassage.
Eyelest, glasseye yetest.
Eyerhyme, sightful urime.
Eyeself, aworn isocket.

Eyeselves, emberdied arevisions.
Eyess, twiney seesockets.
Eyeyield, viscual shutterance.

F

Fablebody, mothical fingure.
Facest, ashist suspiracy.
Facetism, twotalitarian ragime.
Facist, oblious prognazi.
Fagend, unendless ashcape.
Famachine, combind airvector.
Faminechine, crombone airvesture.
Faremachine, trombine carvestor.
Farmachination, complianed harvector.
Farmachine, comblind earvestry.
Farmachinery, combone hairvester.
Farmarchine, compine halvaster.
Farmatching, compline arevesper.

Farmechine, hombone disvestor.
Farminechina, combline hairvista.
Faunication, estial zoomulation.
Fealther, distent pollumage.
Fearfly, flittoral scarwing.
Fearther, dastant seebird.
Featherending, therminal quillity.
Featherhood, rarental avice.
Fedgehund, timemitted fecond.
Feelign, bewhisked catacosmos.
Feeligng, sententient furfeal.
Feelimb, tractile legendarm.
Feheather, rarental shefather.
Felame, torchestral firenzy.
Ferather, birdly legendarm.
Fermelt, yeastern urmoil.
Fervolity, inebrile anaticism.
Feverending, inebrile ashakes.
Fielday, articular campsight.
Filigreen, copperite teeracery.
Fingure, fleshish rinjury.
Finitem, endles onsumption.
Finjury, fishfingered sheark.
Finnegan, begin against.
Firarm, needley treemament.
Firemament, mordial felame.
Firescape, braniched treegress.
Firescrape, vulcanic erention.
Firmamelt, laquid oozean.
Firstation, fier rengine.

Flabberghost, shroudead rejectoplasm.
Flameflower, napalmy blastom.
Flawchart, suspicted craction.
Fleshelf, meatrical embodimelt.
Fleshleash, owlpale eyess.
Flighth, windwinged aetherplane.
Flitre, bucic pacacity.
Florest, marketring flowceller.
Florever, purennial erose.
Florifice, lowerful oppening.
Flowerflow, apline meladow.
Flowever, shallways lowfest.
Flowrest, belloming riverser.
Foarmed, is fwarmed.
Fogetherness, hazelying togethernest.
Fondlingerer, grosping manhand.
Fondlingerie, fingurious belaciness.
Footplath, trackles Byronway.
Forecester, descentient wealther.
Foreinger, bringed staranger.
Foreknication, cutlerious indutery.
Forelegend, armid protomyth.
Foremother, downbearing marecestor.
Foreshorest, beechy teetrop.
Forespost, anteafter prepast.
Forestament, yearlier inkarnation.
Forestand, clearfeeled lumberness.
Forestare, regetated woord.
Forestatement, perevious ashelf.
Foretc, woulden canopty.

Forknication, proronged lovertine.
Forknife, portmantic cluttlery.
Formfrom, ormless wierld.
Forsty, muddleaged crumbfort.
Fraguile, selvered brokenning.
Freedome, aternal giberty.
Frequenzy, fiteful epilens.
Frequest, oftentative shearch.
Freudalism, unsureal seminature.
Friskylark, flitteral fellight.
Fritful, lushlily parakeatsian.
Frogfrond, popool splashash.
Froghorn, toaddled notemission.
Frogleap, amphibranched upond.
Frogmance, insistuous prinkiss.
Frogmancy, aquid foretune.
Frogmanship, iamphibian pondcraft.
Frogmant, jumpled derivination.
Frogment, anglegged sportion.
Frogpond, splashile frondbreak.
Frogrespond, damphibian echorus.
Frogspond, tadpolar marginaliens.
Frogsporn, thighly foreneckate.
Frogsprawn, membryonic tidepolarity.
Frotheather, lathery ratherhood.
Frothmother, wavespun seaset.
Frotht, icyspun seaspume.
Fumiform, chaoshaped pelessness.
Furest, foment unrest.
Furitful, anothing nothere.

Furmament, feelign cathair.
Furneral, urnreal brunial.
Furthere, onely toraveller.
Furtherer, heily rictator.
Fword, abscene repletive.

G

Gabrage, ittery carstore.
Gangreenery, riotten exlimb.
Garagerage, aganst diing.
Garganticline, gemorphic sinkline.
Gauntee, eskeletal bebard.
Gazel, twisthorned antelode.
Gealm, golemlike falme.
Gelans, prenile cementia.
Gendalarm, poolice ificer.
Genderarm, ragent gestaple.
Gene, et alia.
Genet, sais quoi.
Genitalian, gonaddled monstar.
Genitalien, beastirred oregan.

Genitalman, escortly olover.
Genitalmud, asemitic bioble.
Geomorpheme, overbal oroteny.
Ghoul, ghost's soul.
Giacometry, legenthened effigures.
Girlfried, stired lovern.
Globlet, lobely grale.
Gloseme, underfined verstatement.
Glossaxon, golemic ebowulf.
Glosseme, meanfest syllabar.
Glosseye, ornagraphic malegazine.
Glossuary, extenglish bonelist.
Glost, longly preparition.
Glottary, lessical rechord.
Gloveinsect, deantlered thumbug.
Glug, bathtub plughole.
Godmoth, antennable feartherer.
Godsong, evensent hyman.
Gohost, ephemereal unset.
Goldense, heardend metality.
Golemdawn, clayborn yeasterday.
Gonesong, longong songtorment.
Gongtorment, yeastian faroth.
Gorave, tombedded urnament.
Grandmoth, hoverarching flauterer.
Grazelle, twicorned zelbra.
Greenereye, innermoist jelosity.
Groanmother, allbearing bearther.
Gruburbs, hiving beestobe.
Guantanimal, cubanned encagement.

Gullcluster, swanswarm crowcloud.
Gulleye, seager orifish.
Gunsinger, weastern sharriff.

H

Habitacle, tempural agoda.
Hairafter, baldeer's lossophy.
Halfinch, fullinch chaffinch.
Halfucinate, seethis limage.
Halpenis, venful genitalien.
Hamunburger, pateyed bunmeal.
Hendengine, stempowered farmachine.
Handgel, misturizing palmoistry.
Handsolo, onanymous starwarrior.
Handynasty, footbound manchinery.
Hangeling, infantast globlin.
Hapenis, heavenspent groater.
Harmacy, veinvasive hemistery.

Harmth, hostly damange.
Harpdiscord, clanghourous uproaratorio.
Hastorian, textial prewriter.
Hauntiquarian, untique antity.
Hawhawk, predating headversary.
Hawthrone, crowcrowned seathedge.
Hazelight, catkind corpice.
Headand, embodiless houlder.
Headarch, overuling monorch.
Headdress, veloped hathat.
Headhold, nostrial sucket.
Headhole, earful eyeleak.
Headitor, incipial roofreader.
Headress, ashionable flowear.
Headressed, aboding esident.
Headroom, bedruminous hamber.
Headrust, dissupporting invalaid.
Headsettle, lauditory ucination.
Headstrang, nonecked mulever.
Headstring, betied hatholder.
Headstrung, isloyal structer.
Hearbeat, prepulsive earroar.
Heardbeat, tomtummy monodrone.
Hearse, she arse.
Hearsederiver, undertalking ballpearer.
Hearsedrawn, pallid coffinery.
Hearteach, listend breathart.
Hearteat, shuckling earbeat.
Heartesian, cogmatic thinkengine.
Hearthread, wereby willcome.

Hearthwork, amparted houstle.
Heartwork, omental pullabour.
Heavant, etcarian rainsect.
Heavenery, mangelic sexecration.
Heavent, ecclecelestial paravice.
Heaverafter, alofted sluicide.
Hedgefund, amental misvestment.
Hedgehodge, spikeful irrodent.
Hedgehund, stockbroke lichense.
Hedgemoney, heavenspent sedgefund.
Helicopterror, bladed autopile.
Hemicolon, unctuated paraphaph.
Hemistry, coalchemical lalembic.
Hemlet, heedlocked trahedy.
Hemother, vengendered leviathane.
Hemystery, meldominated doppelgang.
Henceward, swinged hinge.
Henchant, cluckwork glayer.
Heory, unifield thighery.
Hereditorator, rebatable speechking.
Herewolf, lupely furforeal.
Hermenaut, spacemantic interpenetrer.
Herwolf, wehere flowl.
Heterogloss, theretical manyscript.
Hewere, theery airabouts.
Hierattic, lower seller.
Hindcough, dispray atissue.
Hisher, either oreal.
Hiss, and hearse.
Hlisten, shlight unsound.

Homethanks, domestick hostalgia.
Homethinks, funishing monogogue.
Homicider, inkfluenced dreath.
Homorifice, frontoor hopening.
Honeycosm, hummin beeing.
Hophazard, rabitual burrowings.
Horifice, sicketted headhole.
Hornest, beest pollency.
Hornymoon, wanwax experiod.
Horrorscope, stareyed orachle.
Hospiral, veinfected deisize.
Hostorian, minervan scripe.
Hoteliology, motellic roomervice.
Househole, ventual windown.
Hugoball, daedal antimaker.
Hum, a nbeing.
Humdram, stilled whiskeye.
Humean, causal boeing.
Humeanbeing, nomanic onentity.
Humear, laughalong woundtrack.
Humsphere, lullabylike hemis.
Humument, altared blook.
Husted, crowned flaureate.
Hymnself, choreal mindentity.
Hyphenomenon, emdash hemicolon.

I

Iceslur, igloomy slabode.
Ickinsect, twiglegged stickery.
Ictionary, illexical wordbk.
Ideath, definal conslept.
Idleaf, springed grainery.
Idleave, fallable veinery.
Iece, fragminced uruin.
Ieces, its ragments.
Ight, eep arkness.
Ightblub, candlescent filameant.
Ignorphan, unslung ninfant.
Ilduce, mussly lampfruit.
Ilducement, bebribed muscline.
Illight, tumnal eveining.

Illinduce, preductive farschist.
Illive, rearriving deapture.
Ilsand, ninsular marena.
Imaginair, sunsky hearseer.
Imaginationalism, lobal commutiny.
Imaginging, ellusive himsong.
Imagitate, illstirred thourt.
Imagitation, crestless flancy.
Imaglot, etalic motherflicker.
Imanager, rintending eyeboss.
Imirage, ormir orrim.
Imitimotions, of moretotality.
I'mmaterial, flashly ombeddiment.
Immuscle, illducive faschrift.
Imperson, or ality.
Impersonata, chamberred heresong.
Imvagination, vulcanic erupture.
Incarnivore, meateatering aeligature.
Incestor, britten kindread.
Incestore, thinbred urchildren.
Inchcape, coheren't caostline.
Inchscape, nescapable innertitude.
Inclouden, heventh seaven.
Incomple, unfish fragmeant.
Ind, was tinguishable.
Indentity, selfloss mapparition.
Index, contentable consumee.
Indus, trial revolution.
Industreal, preductive cemoddity.
Indwell, nervetheless meltality.

Infantinity, middend finility.
Infinight, enunding ungodown.
Infotain, elevisual introvertisement.
Infotaint, sustraining papaganda.
Ingland, poddy bolitick.
Inheren't, nothereal mothing.
Inlovestment, inescapital sharange.
Innumerubble, postunclear uruins.
Inself, herent outdentity.
Insideity, amnyone's excreation.
Insidentity, nameone's descreation.
Intangibbet, imanginary meater.
Intelligentle, fleeling throught.
Interiornational, insultar patiotism.
Internat, ornation ality.
Intimatter, untimate acrobot.
Intime, enternal stoneself.
Intimidations, of dimortality.
Intomotions, of insectality.
Intricacery, tendrilled revegetation.
Invalady, misladle intangelement.
Inverture, bemusical operature.
Investore, headjusted hairshoulder.
Invision, slightful atorm.
Inword, privatic lasagnage.
Inwordly, selfmost mindhead.
Irror, fulllength headmirer.

J

Jabberjockey, herseriding nonsonsong.
Jaberror, elblowed pushtake.
Jagular, fastalking catskin.
Jambone, tombined maldade.
Janglage, illulated nomebody.
Janglion, brainverted langaugh.
Janguage, clingual illphony.
Janguar, predating panthfinder.
Jejaculate, jaccuse jaccurse.
Jellybeing, quantiquaking fleshelf.
Jellyroll, illgot mermalade.
Johnsense, dictioned glossability.
Johnsensical, chamblic lexiphant.
Johnsonese, nononsensed sententiety.

ohnsong, comeonsense culplet.
Johnsonsense, nonand onsense.
Joinsense, enmerge jumblend.
Joyce, jocoserial revoyce.
Joyceanic, seasensed overseans.
Joyceanyway, wakelier prolexis.
Joycely, finelegantly waked.
Joycense, instensical lilteracy.
Joycescene, impaginated anglexicon.
Joycese, colludic ninesense.
Joycestick, infineganite worldpay.
Joycetick, oyceanic stairage.
Jumblend, comixed turnbable.
Jumpiter, boluncing saggiant.
Jumpstartle, carride awade.

K

Karmachanic, handymantic cancarer.
Kand, insky scraper.
Kerflop, pogfronded rassonance.
Kestreal, ravitating windfuck.
Kingdom, death's dream.
Kingkongdom, unitive progenation.
Kneelbow, ajointed dubble.
Kniverse, metalmorphic tinespace.
Knottier, untiered shotlace.
Knowflake, astormed beleaf.
Knowstorm, imparticled felakes.
Krakawake, violcanic erupture.

L

Laborynth, demazed openeplan.
Laburynth, peneplan irkplace.
Laceswing, beribbed greenerfly.
Ladidada, gagged sungstress.
Lafterlife, posthumerous istence.
Lalanguage, leslang emotif.
Lamblast, pastirred muttilation.
Lambplight, baabarous chophorror.
Language, actually existing.
Languagh, actruely presisting.
Languauge, achtually rexisting.
Languish, acutally exusting.
Langurge, arctually sexisting.
Langyrinth, azamazed parenthesistence.

Laybyrinth, rodecide tipstop.
Learedward, jumblied invator.
Learese, malcolious nonsunsong.
Leathergy, skintire exhast.
Lemangent, unguant leman.
Lexiconoclast, langimage broker.
Lightblub, tuttered flashlife.
Lighttipped, tight-lipped.
Likequid, viscious lightclot.
Lilteral, silant defact.
Lipquid, achewed papulace.
Lipsquid, mealted teaeater.
Littleme, egodly minitaur.
Locean, fissurish abyssure.
Lollopop, cherubby liplover.
Longagog, gazemazed ozement.
Longong, belliful revertebration.
Longsong, evereverberating gongsong.
Longuage, moth urtongue.
Look, inhere yes.
Losslieder, illyric ursona.
Lostranslate, mist intrastation.
Lovedearth, scar city.
Lovelocity, timesung flamily.
Lovestment, defunded funuture.
Lullayby, rodecided slumbar.

M

Machinature, autumnotive archtexture.
Madestroy, desecreated preduct.
Madmanship, carazy unacy.
Magitation, imunagible armage.
Magmanimal, lavaic wolflower.
Mal, edom innate.
Mal, larde imaginaire.
Maldelaire, polpoet maludit.
Maldemur, remporised wallend.
Malegazine, preposterotic sexecration.
Malengender, miscreaked offspiring.
Malkind, animor inimate.
Malladeer, illyric gazel.
Mallard, image inaire.

Malthusiast, opulous maninfestation.
Managenial, bossly temployer.
Mananger, scofficious pluperiority.
Manchine, inimated menguin.
Manchinery, atumated asterslave.
Mangager, prodect spurvisor.
Mangear, apenile pendage.
Manmoth, haired autumoon.
Manuscrypt, bluried unhand.
Manyscript, palimpsestuous heterogloss.
Marinetti, fluturist maninfestor.
Masoschism, intimaterial painfliction.
Masoschist, woundtracked invalaid.
Massmediate, broodcast coreporter.
Meanderth, perimitive riverter.
Meanderthal, imitive romagnon.
Meatal, I amchine.
Meatery, fetarian consumeror.
Megaegg, coval oostritch.
Melancosmic, spacely urnhappiness.
Memebrain, encloded mimessage.
Memor, tremory passionote.
Menace, a trois.
Meremember, lochlost spond.
Merz, schwittery cabollage.
Metaforest, unimagined thetreescape.
Metallurge, alloyed wingscale.
Midden-english, emphemeral ganguage.
Midlust, dustmade mundist.
Mightingale, song blurred.

Mildweed, allgall precess.
Mindwindow, immagerial nonsentity.
Miniataur, theuseless collabyrinth.
Mirrimage, irreflected depicture.
Mirrordoor, opended irreflection.
Mist, ran slate.
Misterbate, motelowning shelfabuser.
Misterror, arcluded pseudpsod.
Mistissue, undisound theresay.
Mistrake, isprint errort.
Mistraker, imparticled ashifter.
Mistshapen, eelemental monstroom.
Misuniverse, orgasmasked precincess.
Monhument, bluried remoans.
Monologoose, fastalking prodent.
Mononcle, avocular unclerity.
Monumetal, brozen iffigy.
Moonglot, phonophone rattelite.
Moonslash, newmorn brackt.
Moonunit, unlit spuntnik.
Moretotality, irrevent outself.
Mortotality, desessed obeing.
Mothes, and monoseism.
Mothing, wingly darksetter.
Mothmother, twowinged eglayer.
Motoray, dustward umbible.
Moundergrowth, jungular frillock.
Mountinside, rainternal chalmber.
Mueslim, edeble breakfaster.
Murmurust, decayed urmur.

Music, or kestrel.
Musoleum, unstiffed seemetary.
Muterror, adumstruck resilence.
Muttersprach, othertongued womanguage.
Myselves, enterelated impersonae.
Mythfire, pallel unverse.
Mythts, seasong of.

N

Nachtingale, midnit songstar.
Namesis, frateful dustiny.
Nameslake, omastic repond.
Namething, no unsubstantive.
Napsalm, singesonged fireharm.
Nauseasick, unwelling vomist.
Nauthsea, wavely betide.
Nauture, versus unture.
Nearcosis, tentranced belivian.
Nearcotic, derugged torance.
Necropolice, cementary angents.
Nemesystem, derangled furries.
Nervending, termined fingerund.
Nervert, trancegressed paraphile.

Nerverted, pathlic gangloon.
Nestleg, teetropped eggend.
Networld, cannected workwide.
Nevendor, veintorn leafeel.
Neverywhere, omnipast poresence.
News, bullet in.
Nightfail, shimmaterial shadowash.
Nighthades, avernal dreapth.
Nightingle, nookturnal solongbird.
Nightingmare, clockturnal singale.
Nightinhale, beareth openairs.
Nightinhaler, lunglulled sungstress.
Nightrain, owlwet tricktack.
Nobaddy, bodilease dancestor.
Nocturine, bladdering prostation.
Nocturntable, redisked shonata.
Nodebody, valved ganglioness.
Nomanimal, roboticant terrormite.
Nomanimalism, apprehensile unnature.
Nomanisan, is land.
Nomanism, belettered particicle.
Nomartisan, marketing startegy.
Nominalasm, wreckaged submachinery.
Nominationalism, urtopian ontopoeia.
Nominazism, englandangered supermicide.
Nomindalism, indeciphered membrain.
Nominimalism, irreductive barenest.
Nominister, staturated yesminster.
Nonaminal, dimbodied exdream.
Nonaminate, amoured terrormite.

Nonimalism, disemvoiced dovedetail.
Nonsensong, insensing subsensong.
Nonsonsing, prevoked porosepoem.
Nooneday, resert shunshine.
Nopedestrian, depaved carway.
Norminalism, neuromantic contradition.
Notebookese, cribbled manyscript.
Nothinged, disc onection.
Nudeparture, bearthed nonentry.
Nudescending, as tearcase.
Nuggot, lavalic gremstone.
Numbor, alterlate dignit.
Numburial, humed effigility.
Numinalism, yeastian imachination.
Nunclear, auncly lavuncle.

O

O, verse timulation.
Obsclarity, belinded ruinsight.
Obsclure, ashadowed inspite.
Oh, verse ear.
Oillspill, blackneed caostline.
Olinger, ringfingery funflinger.
Omewhere, dimstant shome.
Omputer, softing humware.
Onanymous, nonamed massteur.
Onedry, unindundated moonuscript.
Oneirotic, remagined infantasy.
Onelessness, swamb twogether.
Onesday, twomorrow Turday.
Oneselves, doable pronounciation.

Onified, flied othery.
Ontimations, of nomortality.
Oozy, submachine gum.
Opalcity, urband orchitecture.
Operoar, tenorist bomblast.
Or, a cle.
Oralcohol, invitro veritas.
Orchasm, bulbular flowerring.
Orchasmic, embodily precipuce.
Orgasmash, costpoital endres.
Orgasmask, bloodforsaken consecretion.
Orientalisman, fareastern racelet.
Orind, speeled furit.
Orose, tremorseful eregret.
Orpheuse, ythical descendancer.
Ospace, atomniotic undream.
Other-in-law, irrelated kinfold.
Othing, nothinglike ovoid.
Oulipoverty, constrainted poematic.
Outcarnation, manifleshed epiphoneme.
Outdustry, inverterminal ashets.
Overarchitect, gorand destigner.
Oversea, satanzaic scrossing.
Ownershipowner, oiltanked monopolice.

P

Painside, neverevitable illumess.
Paleasure, handgelic sentensation.
Paleasurer, tautosexual onandon.
Paletter, inpaginated secript.
Palmincest, sexfingered plasturbation.
Panglossary, readearly listesse.
Parakeats, consummative lilyschism.
Parakeatsian, chromantic forefeather.
Partocular, nowbound yesight.
Parttern, gulllike seametry.
Paste, prescient furnurture.
Paulcelain, drelicate clockery.
Payphoneme, evocal hearate.
Pearvert, fruitive plome.

Peniscript, snowburnt pissflower.
Penumbrella, cliptic unquell.
Personata, amusic plawyer.
Petal, et al.
Phantomlip, hostly pokesman.
Philosphor, orescent sofist.
Phoneher, phonethem phoneme.
Planest, everevolving scattelite.
Planetrip, discontinental fighlt.
Plathos, morital sluicide.
Playgoround, crotating orchild.
Plushover, upholster downhalter.
Plython, figurtive serepent.
Poembalm, edgar aven.
Poisondart, featherdart objetdart.
Poseproem, porefacial threndition.
Povertry, noninnative autherror.
Povetry, haven't garde.
Prenoir, postnoir Renoir.
Prosepoem, justifiable lineverse.
Prosingsong, mimetrical hepsalm.
Protocopy, xeroxed mimeme.
Protononsense, infarnt belabble.
Protonotion, oceanal reincidence.
Protopoem, pulpoetic overse.
Proverbia, aphoristed coregion.
Prynneval, ageode pindear.
Psychoplath, quazinasi poemaker.
Pulllover, emberace clungingly.
Pushlover, ambrace lungingly.

Q

Qualcify, nameslicked coalchemist.
Qualifly, exampled coinsect.
Quantiquarian, yesteryearn tocktaker.
Quantiquity, depast uruin.
Quarket, atomless urticle.
Quasilazy, missoliny tyraint.
Quasinazi, wightring quotalitarian.
Quastify, substant nonething.
Quastity, inghabited substrance.
Questatement, trest mistament.
Questation, most stament.
Quicksandwich, footheld quakewalk.
Quicksliver, meltal amercury.
Quiltiness, somothering wharmth.

Quiverb, trainsitive flexeme.
Quostatement, mistest statesmelt.
Quostation, recited stament.
Quotality, asinazi fascitation.
Quotestion, ascited mestament.

R

Rainharm, forthe duckie.

Raininglass, staindoors soneday.

Ramessages, papyrusted sqrolls.

Randompage, aeioulian hearp.

Rawtext, onverse reverbiage.

Readeress, readdress searedness.

Readjust, just read.

Readymeal, preaten repasta.

Reboot, rowboat robot.

Referfly, allustrated sciensect.

Refraing, lullabylike dreamsonnet.

Remaindeer, rendosed slantler.

Remembrane, miniscent coretext.

Repulsar, stellar staller.

Retrogarde, postgrade salavage.
Revergreen, everenverduring renfuse.
Reversong, riversing pulsatisfaction.
Revocabulary, submissile statemate.
Rictionary, Johnsensical eference.
Rigormortician, stiffended deadshifter.
River, shiver sliver.
Riverent, effluent dishcharge.
Rivers, silver drivers.
Riverse, selver shelver.
Riverun, unirever seriver.
Rolloll, loorolled ollour.
Roomcervix, hotile alundress.
Rootfoot, rhizoned toetangle.
Roteatery, spoked kebaby.
Rubberst, condomed poregnation.
Rubrick, contructed bloodletter.

S

Sadstone, reeroded untain.
Saehorse, return tossender.
Salarave, indentered wageslaver.
Salavery, alleyed carcareer.
Sandand, seaspreyed ospray.
Sandland, wetless aregion.
Sandwhich, sighn lasagnage.
Sandwithstanding, seaseized bealch.
Sapring, blossomewhere aprising.
Saprising, marchian treemaze.
Saprung, smer autumoon.
Saptimber, autumnail sealson.
Saturay, weakend mistissue.
Saturntable, ervolving playnet.

Saturseven, saturate saturnine.
Savagerage, burbarian apostrocity.
Savagerage, genoble mananger.
Scaffoldil, wallflowered facewound.
Scapescape, scenescent nessness.
Scarabble, bleetlish inutilegame.
Scarletter, redlit crimsonnet.
Scartissue, wanded filesh.
Scenescence, alzheimerical absense.
Scenesence, surrepetitious timeslash.
Scentrail, meastly animalcule.
Schememe, machinatural planot.
Schwa, unphatic glossum.
Schwitter, merziful collagenerator.
Scienescence, perimental fieldage.
Scroll, sea dead.
Seacreation, seminatural demidemon.
Seacreatury, of state.
Seacretion, pulsated materway.
Seashorse, waversed horsea.
Seassault, beachheaded bridgethread.
Seaxchange, regendear tideling.
Secreation, naturinal ompulse.
Seculpture, grayard menument.
Seemen, navalgazing matelots.
Segnegation, Parthic evictory.
Semantelope, demeant glazel.
Semanticant, signsisting instext.
Semebody, rememed fleash.
Semimetaphor, similing orallegory.

Seminature, data basemen.
Semisimile, masterslave singign.
Senseaccordion, subbable touchpouch.
Severybody, sheminated sperman.
Shakesperiment, inheren't anguage.
Shamenace, sheepshifting wolfmankind.
Shaperson, siftshifting prophector.
Sheahorse, undersee oversteer.
Shearse, cardrawn horsebox.
Sheather, ethery dray.
Shecretury, herpent beshemoth.
Sheman, hemistical demiurge.
Shememe, semenstrual shawoman.
Shemonster, krakawake beshemoth.
Shemother, aternal pregenitor.
Sheraphael, cherubbed orchangeling.
Shoppingmal, consuming nilness.
Shrubub, privetted holmland.
Signicism, dissenced capitalisman.
Silfish, insectic sliverrer.
Siltslit, riverfanned midelta.
Simulant, revirtual peppill.
Skeletine, chitinny infect.
Skeletongue, fleshleft combonation.
Skylarkin, highwindow unbard.
Slerpent, inhisspitiable ondrag.
Slilver, ivery nicklace.
Slowly, lowly owly.
Smokesman, immedial newsrepresenter.
Snests, was ps.

Sng, indefindable thomesing.
Snowflak, hindblown icefelt.
Snowowl, lowwinged flollower.
So, andso andsand.
Soleep, drearm reams.
Solong, unsung loansong.
Somebone, hamborn unbody.
Sometimeplace, notheory awhere.
Sometimeteor, unitimate tocometime.
Spiider, reweaving orthrobpod.
Sporm, unfirmed starm.
Sporn, obscenic screan.
Spunknik, orbsorbiting spertilizer.
Stagnantler, bicorned herdress.
Stamm, er er.
Starchamber, grudgemental inquisician.
Starlatan, astrangent statesmelt.
State, fundead terrorvision.
Statesmeant, estatic nomarch.
Statusesque, meatphysical clould.
Stepp, eingston ehenge.
Stickfigurge, scartooned hangelman.
Stigmasks, thrustable tininesses.
Stillbreath, belunged insprint.
Stonehence, polylithic archtexturge.
Suberg, omelting glassier.
Subhubbub, unullutated urmur.
Subsensong, uninterpretable tristrance.
Sugarplump, overaten welfairy.
Sulnight, brimstoned mananger.

Summerse, swesty seaset.
Sungdew, aubeaded wanchorus.
Sunglight, celestated torchson.
Sunriset, mondaily occlosure.
Sunsong, singsong sensing.
Suntzu, Sunra sunrise.
Suptimber, tempiternal sleeptimbre.
Suspident, threadeagled spuntangle.
Suspider, spunended stuckinsect.
Swingbinlid, panshut diesposal.
Swungsong, slunging singsongsense.

T

Tantoncle, plumed minocle.
Taretaker, dustrimmed suspider.
Tautanology, syllabist dislogic.
Tavernacle, tombescent allhell.
Teetrop, rockabraid blaby.
Telescrape, as tronomer.
Telether, unfeeable distrance.
Terevision, dreamsung bloodletter.
Tesco, n sumer.
Texit, egressive caperoute.
The, or em.
Thearth, moonslashed planetheart.
Thearthreat, lobal worming.
Theatearth, globall woreming.

Theaterror, inertial actonement.
Theogamyjig, godleafed thingdom.
Therain, thes now.
Therepy, hereforced rescure.
Therethreat, hitchclocked tyrector.
Therevelation, patmospheric herevision.
Therevision, nomantic heresite.
Thin, gin itself.
Thinglacier, tretreating poledge.
Thisis, antithisis sincethisis.
Thissue, scavernous rarefice.
Thithery, laways ashlant.
Thoughtalogy, nomentalist uncident.
Thoughtology, totalost tautality.
Threadearth, seacreative riveruin.
Threadth, longwinding deathshed.
Threatearth, displanetary cantastrophe.
Threaterre, mondial globility.
Threel, e.g. gedrace.
Thunder, understand sand.
Tie, stablishment an.
Time, a chine.
Timeachine, postfuturist unitraveller.
Timeconsumer, hourglassed suspender.
Timegazine, fleatured airticle.
Timehenge, stonelying recallender.
Timehinge, unjambed doerway.
Timelist, lossarial justment.
Timeocean, workflowed hourself.
Timepaste, thickend quantiquity.

Timescope, retroacting hourgloss.
Timeservant, emporising distator.
Timeslash, rechoherent noughtmare.
Timesoil, spiolt coverlay.
Timesponge, soakular flunnel.
Timesponger, absorbeing dishwaster.
Timestrain, quential carrage.
Timetabolism, billogical earthbeat.
Timeverse, univoiced linegage.
Timewoof, warped dogday.
Tincantation, tancantankerous utroar.
Tingale, anigh sungbird.
Tintangible, authurian ouchstone.
Tinternabulation, sworthian rememberror.
Tirralyrical, tennisung muterror.
Tombalone, scholitory headsphone.
Tongueglue, gluttal strop.
Toothpost, guacamolar milteeth.
Treassurechest, chielf seacreatury.
Treeclump, hillocked glandmark.
Tristanunt, isold losslieder.
Tristranslator, irreversing songfold.
Troubladour, villonous griotard.
Trumour, canclear faucity.
Twisticle, gonaddled imballance.

U

Ubergine, bowl-egged vengetable.
Uhsure, alconfident meanifest.
Unautumn, twiglit treemorse.
Unchild, minatural urchimp.
Uncling, auntic stickingsect.
Uncurl, toms carbine.
Uncyclopedia, tristranslable webverse.
Undecipher, scorolled papyrust.
Underarrestimate, destain clawfully.
Undernearth, misinterred pretator.
Underthunder, thendering wounderender.
Underword, nexpressed subverb.
Unevening, seagulled curflew.
Unfern, farlong refinial.

Ungel, herub dreamon.
Unicon, invertexed icorn.
Uninhabitant, innavitive doweller.
Uninverse, opposight mirrimage.
Unireverse, timeravelling oceantropy.
Unirhyme, unipoetry universe.
Unnature, uprose inverse.
Unriver, univer reveruin.
Unset, sune sunriset.
Unshore, handlocked bereach.
Unsurection, nonvolent irrevolution.
Untidictionary, glosslost exicon.
Untilitarian, waithing telostness.
Untimations, of amortality.
Unverse, prosely ordorder.
Unwin, downwindow aircon.
Unwinable, managled descomposition.
Unwince, sensewim uneverbabble.
Unwind, unlost falanguage.
Unwindow, oplaque vowelcabulary.
Unwinese, urticulate babblelong.
Unwinian, nonjohnsonian senselist.
Unwinism, hearsaid remarquees.
Unwins, dictiony intertainers.
Unwinsense, lullabide janglage.
Upsided, own ership.
Urpoem, seminal versical.
Utterbly, chainged utterbly.
Utterflight, twowinged allustration.
Utterflown, slilent shutterer.

V

Vaginasaur, vulvatic wombearth.
Vehicicle, farozen cartrack.
Veinsect, shewing lacewind.
Veintrance, needlied narcoterie.
Verblist, lexative dictationary.
Verdose, glaxosmith cline.
Verseas, joyceanic mocean.
Versel, satanzaic crimsecheme.
Verself, paraphable designition.
Versestatement, poembalmed slimile.
Verstatement, noetic liesense.
Vertebrain, hazeheaded cereberus.
Verticing, cervicing crevicing.
Videosyncrasy, youtubular nighthades.

Villon, lastest ament.
Virality, memely sporead.
Virgilante, ravant garde.
Vivinsect, chitinny glacewing.
Vivisible, invirgible isvisible.
Volcabulary, extinglished verbalance.
Volcayes, adoryes hurricayes.
Voneme, dreadly mightshade.
Vortext, avantic embryody.
Voyear, yoyour isight.
Vwlssnss, consonantial clck.

Warfart, violint shruggle.

Warsp, stingly hornest.

Wartorment, battleflied recretation.

Wastime, istime cometime.

Wateriality, of signifier.

Wavenus, seaspraysprung ideity.

Waxend, ringfingerthin toerapper.

Well-defined, well defiled.

Whalesolong, spacific oceanaria.

Wharfare, world whyed.

Whealth, inhurted treamure.

Whereforest, treeringed thicknet.

Whereoscope, musoleum paperodox.

Wind, blotch maker.

Windowl, forshaken preyer.
Wolflow, babaying earwulf.
Wolfox, vixing dogmachine.
Womanhole, mentrancing engress.
Wordbk, wierld glossuary.
Wordead, tear mination.
Wordliest, bodlied demisurge.
Wordloss, glosslist neverb.
Wordraw, lobal cornflict.
Wordroot, worldriven etcetymon.
Wordslip, triptongued vocableed.
Wordsway, overtherealist reveriething.
Wordswere, tinternal precurrence.
Wordsword, cromantic egographer.
Wordsworm, slegmented bookurn.
Wordswort, brewers yeats.
Wordward, towardly verblist.
Wordwarp, wellmed meltaphor.
Wordwind, aeoalien wharp.
Workflow, autanimal timemotion.
Worldsend, gravestart avestone.
Wreninch, bierd immeasure.

Xecutive, mangagerial salareme.
Xdream, midwoke alarmblast.
Xenagogue, afforeign suspeaker.
Xenogloss, marginalien tonguestem.
Xenoglossary, entropped worldist.
Xenophone, othertongued nodebody.
Xeroxer, protocopy manchine.
Xstream, draughted deriverbed.
Xtremes, of consciousness.

Y

Yawp, blurbaric nonerope.

Yearstirday, revistless kniversary.

Yeastoday, tristilled nowadaze.

Yeatsy, bypass horsamentation.

Yell, ow submine.

Yesight, ivid ision.

Yessirday, ordread moarning.

Yestersecond, momentorn thitherworld.

Yolkfolk, tarday exexaminers.

Yregami, rrorr imagery.

Z

Zentrance, froze editation.
Zeppeling, hinderberg montgolflier.
Zeronought, startravelling astronome.
Zerosity, vacumulant nothering.
Zigzagurat, pyre amidic.
Zilther, wirestrung nonstrument.
Zoomulation, shecreative seamonstress.
Zoonimal, moonheaded azebra.
Zootailors, furbricant suitablist.
Zystem, eyetimized glosses.

Ingram Content Group UK Ltd.
Milton Keynes UK
UKHW010132040423
419518UK00003B/56